POETRY EN PLEIN AIR

Poetry En Plein Air

Marianne Szlyk

Selected and New Poems

POETRY EN PLEIN AIR

© 2020 Marianne Szlyk

Cover art: *America* by Tom Brown
Book layout: Barbara Shaw

ISBN 978-0-9753095-7-5

First Edition

Published by:
Pony One Dog Press
Suite 113
1613 Harvard Street, NW
Washington, DC 20009

To my father, Paul R Szlyk;
my husband, the wry environmental poet, Ethan Goffman;
and our cats, Callie and Thelma McKay.

Contents

Introduction

Marianne Szlyk's poetry, rich in detail and expressed through an astute perception, presents an open invitation into the poet's bustling inner sanctum. Szlyk's very first poem, "The Poet of Spotsylvania," introduces a theme familiar to the tapestry of *Poetry En Plein Air*, the theme of venturing beyond the comfort of the poet's physical sanctuary to endure certain banalities in outside world. The speaker of the opening poem clarifies how she feels:

> I want to stay home
> where my yard grows all
> the words, images, and rhymes
> I need for my poems.
> Nevertheless,
>
> I get in my car
> and drive north to work.
> There strip malls bloom like
> poison puffballs on far-off fields
> that once grew sweet corn.

While the theme of eschewing occasional mendacity that populates the public domain recurs from time to time, the speaker does not, however, remain holed up behind a second story window overlooking the local cemetery. In fact, she ventures beyond her sanctuary quite often. Numerous poems reference locations both local and regional so one quickly realizes that intellectual curiosity transcends the desire for static security. Along the way, Szlyk's ability to detail accurately her journey to places near and far becomes evident throughout every linguistic twist and turn. Szlyk's lexicon is detailed, intricate and riddled with imaginative insight. Her metaphors, complex yet accessible, encourage readers to experience her intellectual and emotional journey. One observes how each poem focuses upon the details of the moment at hand. The sentiment of each poem feels genuine and not manufactured for convenience. William Blake said, in so many words, that a fool sees not the same tree that a wise man sees. He meant, of course, that poets must focus as individuals upon the world of concretes and not acquiesce to an artificial world of concepts for convenience. Szlyk's concretes are astute and arresting. At times figurative concretes are summoned to articulate. Notice from her poem, "Narrow," when she says "In this part of the country, / windows narrow, // squeezing sunlight into the bedroom / as if it were lemon juice" or from "Summer Solstice on U Street" we encounter "The scent of mango dusted with / chili powder and cinnamon / trickles in with the piano and drums" and from "Chicory," "I stay strong / when the air is like bus exhaust / and the sky is a dull ache."

If you ask Marianne Szlyk about the major influences on her work, she'll tell you that Robert Lowell, Anne Sexton and Elizabeth Bishop are paramount. One can see Lowell's influence through Szlyk's penchant for personal reflection. Her frequent focus upon the faces and names of people in her life come into vision with photographic accuracy to detail the intimate content of her life. Here there is affinity with Lowell in general and Sexton in particular when personal relationships involve tension. But it is Szlyk's ability to perceive with clarity the ordinary and sometimes extraordinary details of day to day existence that binds her to Bishop. Szlyk's unique ability to detail her emotional depth encourages her poems to read like Bishop but feel like Lowell and Sexton.

Throughout *Poetry En Plein Air*, aka, poetry outdoors or in plain sight, one is greeted time and again by at least a hint of what Ezra Pound called for in his treatise on Imagism: "Direct treatment of the thing whether subjective or objective" and "To use absolutely no word that does not contribute to the presentation." Szlyk's lexicon is well-crafted and acutely focused upon many *things*—things which emote the poet's inner life. Through meticulous diction Szlyk invites readers to feel what the poet herself feels, and her descriptions often lead to particular sensations that reveal the tone of her poems. She can soothe: "Sunlight hovers on the left / like the white light of myth, / movies, and musicals." She can arouse: "The ghosts of green papayas / and used bookstores / haunt the chain restaurants / that rise up like / invasive flowers." And she can emote a somber aura: "At night in another strange bed / tiger-striped with streetlights / and shadows of venetian blinds, / the jazz harpist wills herself / to sleep."

Of the many things one can say about the complexity inherent in Szlyk's poetry, one constant is that her poems, rich in detail, reveal with precision the poet's inner life that churns nonstop. One poem, of many to be sure, that captures the remarkable abilities of *Poetry En Plein Air* is "Walking the Former Orange Line":

Wendy walks the spine of the city
made of burnt umber brick
from tenements torn down after fire,
after renewal.

She walks beneath the canopy of unnamed trees
and sees people who look like her.
Two shaven-headed men
play tennis. Sweat glistens
on dark faces and white chests.
A woman, her head covered
in orange, blue, and brown cloth,
pushes her baby stroller past a couple walking dogs.

Wendy reminds herself that this is just a path
from one place to the next, from café to street fair
from school to home, for those who were not born

when this path was an elevated subway,
a scar running down the city's face.

Marianne Szlyk acknowledges many influences. "Walking the For-mer Orange Line," for example, is a persona poem written during her participation in Dr. Michael Anthony Ingram's DC Poetry Project. She cites her affection for Chinese poetry, in particular, Kenneth Rexroth's 1971 anthology, *One Hundred Poems from the Chinese*, as well as interest in the young African-American poets, Tara Betts and Abdul Ali. Szlyk is also quick to mention the influence of her friend, Catfish McDaris, a poet whose own work bears the influence of Charles Bukowski; Reuben Jackson; and, finally, the late great jazz poet, Felino Soriano. That's a re-markable diversity of influences for a poet who is never static, never sat-isfied with past accomplishments, and forever curious. I invite you to enjoy *Poetry En Plein Air* as much as I do.

–Alan Britt, *Gunpowder for Single-ball Poems*
Towson University

From On the Other Side
of the Window

The Poet of Spotsylvania

I scan the afternoon sky
for words, images, rhymes. Birds
take off from grasping trees
to fly south towards dolphins
and palms, towards warm ocean,
the direction I'm not going.

I want to stay home
where my yard grows all
the words, images, and rhymes
I need for my poems.
Nevertheless,

I get in my car
and drive north to work.
There strip malls bloom like
poison puffballs on far-off fields
that once grew sweet corn.

After work, I will not
see or hear the birds
sleeping in the barren trees.
My son will play videogames
behind a locked door. Gunfire

and tinny music will escape,
running upstairs to remind me
he's home. I'll go online

to visit the other poets
back from call centers, hospitals,
strip malls, and truck stops.

Then I'll write my poems.

Abandoned

June bamboo swallows
the bite-sized house. Sharp, green teeth
pierce darkness within.

Rooftop antenna
pulls in static. Red-winged black-
birds perch on its arms.

Humidity blooms
inside and out. Summer rain
curls up in the tub.

Paper coffee cups
clatter on bare floors. Dust
specks rise, caught in webs.

Empty hangers chat-
ter in the bedroom closet.
Bats greet another dusk.

At Mile Zero on SR 26

The open road unspools
like a fresh typewriter ribbon
before even one smack
of a noiseless key
onto heavy, white paper.

You forget that you hate
typewriters, especially
inserting a new ribbon.

Turn on the radio.
Stations weave in
and out
like drivers in city traffic.

You'd settle for silence,
but then the old song
you love best
staggers in beside you,
keeping you company
on the road home.

At the Water's Edge

after Cezanne, "At the Water's Edge" (c. 1890)

Resisting the hot wind, this house at the water's edge
retreats beneath the whir of trees.

Their dry brushstrokes are blue like water or sky
and green as the end of spring.

But mostly they are the colors
of canvas, earth, and parched leaves.

The sky is a haze of brushstrokes, a wash of turpentine,
smoke to the water's edge.

Hills loom behind the house;
they are mirages made of thinned paint.

More buildings appear, shimmers in the haze,
reflections in the water.

No swimmer, no boat breaks the surface,
more mirror for land and sky than home for fish and weeds.

But the house's heart is dark and sweet
with sage and lavender, with the scent of grass and lake

protecting its guests from the hot wind, the drought,
and the smoke to the water's edge.

Maryvale Park in July

The pond at the park clouds over.
Flies and fish kiss the water's surface.
Three birds dart through the air above.

Everywhere there is life in the water,
the reeds, the islands of brown-gray mud,
the flowers that crowd around the pond

as it shrinks and grows opaque. But
I cannot find the turtle I saw
last night. Squinting, holding my breath, I

glimpse it. But it does not move.
It is a turtle-shaped rock, mineral, not animal.
Bronze diamond, it will stay there forever.

I listen to the cicadas' twisting percussion,
look for flowering milkweed, and watch fireflies
like beads of sweat on hot nights.

Soon they too will die. Only sky,
earth, and water will remain.

Seaweed on the Beach

Reds, greens, browns, and mustard yellow,
add earthy undertones,
the taste of miso,
to the neons, the overexposed
blues and whites and yellows,
the painted plaques and t-shirts,
the stick candies and salt-water taffy
sold at the gift store.

The rusty Irish moss
on this beach
will not turn into
anemones or coral
or even amber sea glass.
It lingers like
the seagull accents
wheeling in the wind
past summer.

Looking Out to Spectacle Island in April

The beach this time of year
is nothing but rocks.
She ignores the man
who is placing one
on top of the other,
trying to balance them.

She ignores his dog.

She is waiting for the summer
of bare-chested boys in shallow water,
baseball on the radio,
and the reggae ice cream truck
with its flavors
of soursop, mango, and rum raisin.

She is waiting.

Rocky Mountain High

I don't remember mountains in Denver.
I mistook them for clouds steeped
in shadow, soaked in wind, hugging

the horizon, limiting the distance of
our spectacled vision. Without a car,
the road through the mountains was

something to imagine, not to travel.
I remember walking wide streets, past
empty storefronts and flickering neon cacti.

Cutting through the university quad free
of weeds and students, we talked
about books we'd read and then

strolled to Safeway and the apartment.
I remember watching Seinfeld in black
and white. We drank Crystal Pepsi,

ate toasted bagels, the frozen kind,
smaller than my fist. Cynthia drew the
smoky drapes against night's noise, against

mountains in the distance, the future
of endless beginnings and false starts,
our late twenties, the nineteen nineties.

After Miles Davis' *Amandla*

Metallic trumpet
rises like heat mirages
over cracked asphalt.

Early morning drums
echo like the sidekick's fingers
on his closed window.

Eastern Oregon:
a blank land before breakfast.
Mountains are just haze.

Rainclouds hug the coast,
days away from this road trip.
Keyboards mimic rain.

It will not fall here.
Miles' trumpet scorches white
earth one cannot own.

The Day Before the Bridge Closed

On Boston's Long Island, I walk
over unmarked graves of residents,
now lost in earth and rocks,
hidden like they have always been
at this hospital, in their neighborhoods
before the city gentrified.

I stand at the island's edge,
looking out to waves, empty
space that smells of rot and
seaweed. The ragged tide rolls in
from Spain, leaving green sea glass
on this beach. Seagulls hover
over the prickly waves' unraveling,
over green shards worn smooth.
Tomorrow only ghosts will watch.

Birch Trees in North Carolina

The needle-thin trunks glint
the way the odd, white threads
do in a quilt of blues,
browns, and greens.

I do not recognize other trees,
but I know the birch.
Its peeled bark is snow
clinging to spring.
Its leaves are wind chimes.
Its roots clutch at the stone wall
between long-gone pasture
and forest.

I see this birch in Carolina,
not up north where I expected it,
but here among the rows
of oak and pine, beside
pools of water, part of
this quilt of sky, earth, and vine.

Savannah in January

Yearning for spring, I imagine
Spanish moss as white blossoms
bringing scent and warmth nearer.

I count bright green leaves
but find their waxy shade
impossible to bear in cold.

I seek snowdrops and crocus
but only see drowned camellias
closed to weak, winter sun.

Even here it's not time
for magnolias or cherry trees.
Flowers wait in vases, inside.

Today I circle the fountain
its edges trimmed with ice,
its trim painful to touch.

The Blooms of Fall

The sunburst's orange, rust and brown
burn into a turquoise door.
The last of the day lilies blanch
beneath this clash of color.

Hard green and white shields
armor the street tree.
The moss named British soldiers
musters in the bark below.

Tendrils cling to live oak,
the ghost of Walt Whitman,
lingering where young men at the college
sprawl, play ball, loiter, or loaf.

Other gray strands, the ghost of Li Bo,
dangle from a silver tree to the west.
In its shade, the red-haired scholar
memorizes poetry in Chinese.

A whole world in red, green, gray,
and orange blooms on pieces
of bark from trees fallen in silence,
on rocks made from the beginning of time.

In fall, in miniature, in moss and lichen,
another whole world is still blooming.

Under the Sign of Ash

Just past solstice, we walk out
on Rock Creek Trail. Thin, brittle
ash trees crowd low mounds away
from both the path and water.

I recognize this tree. Its leaves
littered the pool even in summer.
Its branches shattered in spring breezes.
Fall purples and yellows muddied still,
warm waters.

On Rock Creek Trail, green dots
mark each trunk infested with ash
borers. These trees will be cut
down soon.

I imagine this trail without shade
in high summer. Together we watch
the thin creek flow. White bubbles,
the ghosts of leaves, float past.

I review my Celtic astrology. Ash
lives long, rises high, is grounded
by extensive roots. It shelters children.
Its wood becomes cradles. This is
not that world.

Blue Green and Brown (Rothko 1952)

She wonders what is intimate
about an enormous canvas hung
upon a museum wall.
Museums are silent except for
garbled conversations, docents' lectures, spills
of sound from someone's device.
Nothing is intimate, not even
silence, the pristine space between
each person in a public place.

She sits at home with
the image on her screen,
all other lights off. In
twilight, blue, green, and brown
envelop her, keeping her company
in this humidity. Cicadas call
outdoors. Indoor and outdoor sounds
blend: buses' wheeze, the washer's
slosh. She feels the space
between her and them dissolve.

Waleje for Caroline

I.

Gone to seed,
the onion flowers,
purple globes
erect in the wind
that, cooling,
promises rain soon,
no more endless summer.

II.

Banana and Louie bark,
recalling Caroline
to the tasks on her list:
wake the twins dress them feed them
get them into the car drive to the bank
drive to the strip mall buy cigarettes liquor stamps
drive to Lucky buy dog food people food kid food.

III.

Women from her grandmother's day
did not sweat. They glowed.
Her daughters will sweat,
playing tennis to win, lunging for the ball.
Caroline does neither.
Standing, chilled behind the picture window,
she lights a cigarette.

IV.

Caroline imagines the inland empire.
There the fields of onion flowers
extend in all directions
to the two-lane highway
to the forests to the mountains
to the other coast thousands of miles away.
She dreams of striding through these fields.

V.

Stabbing out her unsmoked cigarette,
Caroline turns away from the road
and towards the ocean.
She finger-combs her blonde hair,
too short for babies to yank.
Then she moves as if she were
already wading through saltwater.

VI.

Passing the photographs from Malibu,
she wonders if, like the onions,
she has gone to seed.
She sucks in her stomach
beneath her baggy blouse and shorts.
The dogs follow her.
She praises them but quickens her pace.

VII.
Walking down to the girls' room
with its windows on the beach,
she remembers
wearing yellow
blowing on dandelions
gone to seed
to bring on endless summer.

VIII.
Onion flowers bear with them
the tang of fall. She is now
three years past twenty,
two years a mother.
Come next spring, she promises
to show her twin daughters
dandelions.

IX.
Wagging their tails,
the dogs rush into her daughters' room.
The twins wake up for their friends.
Next spring she and the girls
will blow on dandelions gone to seed
to bring on endless summer
and the onion flowers of fall.

Evening on Washington Street

Walking where city blurs into suburb,
she sees yards of red roses
and orange lilies. Women her age
or older work in rich dirt
while grandchildren play.
Spanish phrases float
in the breeze around her.

Yet she smells nothing but the sweetness
of laundry detergent and fabric softener:
the choking purple fog of lavender grit.

Just off the path she rejected,
a green, peppery scent prevails.
There she could breathe deeply. But
she chose the known. She didn't
know where that path through woods
would have led her in twilight.

She knows the fog will dissolve
before she enters the square
and houses withdraw onto side streets.
She knows the white boxwood flowers
will smell like homemade soap,
cleansing the night as it falls.

Tonic

Chiefly Eastern New England: soda pop

Morning thunderstorms keep us home,
away from swimming lessons and
the round of suburban errands.
Heavy, buggy clouds rumble;
lightning flashes beyond the pines.
Yesterday's humidity still clutches at us.

My mother sends my brother
to the basement to shut off
the electricity. The fan sputters,
then dies. We listen
to a transistor radio.
Jagged static interrupts
last summer's soft rock hits.
I sneak diet ginger ale
before it is tepid and flat.

Next summer I'll be working
for my father in the city
in the air-conditioned,
windowless office
on Dorchester Avenue.
Drinking icy cans of Pepsi
from the corner store,
listening to the Providence station,

I will imagine summer in Seekonk.
It blazes with classic rock
and feels as smooth as coconut oil
while storms keep my brother
and my mother home.

Visiting the Ancestors

The deer are visiting the ancestors,
nibbling on grass at Mt. Calvary,
waiting in the shade of winter

underneath the low trees that could be
on a riverbank in the deep
South that the ancestors fled from.

The five deer browse on the
pale green fringe of the cemetery,
limp parsley left on winter's plate

beside the river that neither flows
nor freezes. The deer have bodies
the color of earth in shadow,

but they could be spirit animals
of family living elsewhere come to
visit great-grandparents in the ground,

the great-grandfather who was gentle with
farm animals, remembered horses and mules,
the great-grandmother who kept a pot

on the stove for family, neighbors,
and friends, served Red Rose tea
with milk and sugar like coffee,

The deer linger on the fringes
like the awkward children they
once were when the ancestors

were alive.

Home from the Oncologist

Parking her car, Thelma counts the crows
balancing on the roof of her house.
The birds are almost as big as chimneys.

She tries to remember the meaning of crows.
Maybe owls or ravens are the auguries
out West where trees tower over houses.

But she knows Van Gogh's last painting,
the murder of crows in the cornfield
a day or two before he died.

She will ask her friends.
She cannot ask her husband.
He's been dead two years.

Thelma watches the crows fly
off to the neighbors' large house.
Crows are just birds up there.

On her roof they loomed like omens
from nights swirling with coal dust and
cigarette smoke, throbbing with nausea,

from another painting whose light
is just a smear of yellow and orange
oils trapped behind black lines.

She pictures her family's ghosts hovering
over her street, trying to find where she lives.
Once they find her, she must join them.

She must become like them,
dust and smoke mingling with crows,
whirling in blue over Vincent's wheat.

At Bonaventure Cemetery

After an image by Mary Judkins

At home in the world,
Spanish moss flows like sunlight
from the trees whose roots
are in fertile ground.
Sunlight hovers on the left
like the white light of myth,
movies, and musicals.

Today the ancestors walk among us,
recognizing the children in the adults,
laughing at the fashion
and gadgets we cherish.

Not at home in the world,
the mourning madonna hugs the cross,
but she is streaked with green.
Even the shadow striping her gown
is the color of soil, the red bricks
of the city beyond. Her tears
are moss, not the bitter crystal
that etches stained glass
and indoor stone.

The ancestors tiptoe around her,
but they mingle with us
in and out of sunlight,
in and out of shadow.

Returning to Jamaica Pond

On this cool day, sunlight
hides behind frayed clouds that
light turns translucent. Dank, green-
brown scent does not rise
from the opaque pond as
it did on warmer days.

After stepping off the outbound
trolley swaying into the future,
I once walked this pond
without stopping, without looking,
without reflecting.

Pausing for breath, I look
out to Turtle Island's rock
over which a dead tree
sprawls. This island is shrinking.
Rising waters will conceal it
long before the ocean covers
this growing city, my grave,
this shrinking grave, my city.

Rothko on Portland Street

Rothko's paintings always make her think
of windows. She is sitting up
one evening in an East Cambridge kitchen,
hours past some man's bedtime, staring
at flat roofs and barbed-wire tangle,
a mile from the river. There
on day-glo afternoons kids her age
row the Charles after beef stir-fry
and before physics homework. She scrapes
butter into a bowl of brown
rice she had cooked, hoping he
would not miss even one grain.

Drinking tap water, wishing for soda,
she studies the Chinese Trees of Heaven
that spring up on Portland Street.
Rothko would have left them out
if he had been painting here.
They are too leafy, their triangles
disturbing the color blocks, their greens
disrupting the wash of orange paint.

Still the view makes her think
of Rothko, the poster she sees
at the college bookstore, the picture
on a book of poetry bought
elsewhere, closer to the river, to
read when she stays home alone.

When Words Are Stones

Standing at the edge of the river,
she looks out at the caramel flood,

its thick, sweet color swelling over where
the stones were last summer. She remembers

seeing them for the first time, noticing
how bright the river was, how many

stones gathered around the stream like words
she could speak here with new friends

in this city, not her own. Choosing
a stone, feeling its dryness, its heat,

she considered whether to throw it or
to bring it to her room. Today

all stones are drowned in dirty water.
Today she has spoken to no one.

The river smells of mud, of drowned,
lost animals caught in the sudden flood

without branches to cling to. A leafless
tree stands aloof, branches out of reach

from water that laps at its roots.
This tree has survived each year's floods.

She turns away, knowing that the stones
will return, that words will, too. Tomorrow

she returns here whether the flood rises
or retreats. Next spring she will watch

it carrying away black branches and corpses
through the heart of this college town.

But today she returns home.

In Pale November

I was Marianne Moore, wearing a black straw hat,
we wandered through the woods she knew too well.

Leafless trees clutched at the faded sky.
Stones and fallen branches littered the ground.

I listened to a youthful harangue
and watched for birds and plants she would have seen,

but it was long past time for even poison ivy
or bittersweet berries. So he and I drifted

until the early dark pooled at our feet
to freeze and trip us like the branches, stones,

and fallen leaves that always cling to pale November.
For years beginning with that month,

I listened to his middle-aged litany and ignored
the leather-bound books she wove into her poetry,

following the sound of his voice
into and through the woods and out the other side

to the early darkness, the evergreen trees,
the stray cats, the bus stop signs like clenched fists,

to the long ride on empty buses
back to the city we always returned to.

Walking through Rock Creek Park in November,
having left the city I always returned to,

I count syllables the way she did.

Narrow

In this part of the country,
windows narrow,

squeezing sunlight into the bedroom
as if it were lemon juice.

In this part of the country,
porches are tiny.

One plant in its terra cotta pot
stands in for coleus and marigolds,

for woods behind the house,
for vacant lots full of Queen Anne's Lace.

In this part of the country,
black cats race down brick alleys.

There is no room for grass
or children.

The Summer After the Bridge Closed

In the absence of lawn mowers, the sparrow's
song flows down slate tiles,
over brick walls and wooden window sills
to the rocks at island's edge.

Fat black crows strut down
quiet streets, across matted grass.
Without hawks or humans,
crows have no need to fly.

Waves crash onto smaller stones
that gather next to the rocks.
The ocean's fingers crumble
the beach as if it were a cracker.

For now, starlings emerge
from rhododendrons and boxwoods.
The birds' notes replace the rain
during this dry summer.

The grass is greener. Clover
mingles with chicory and milkweed.
Long grass sways in the wind.
It flowers.

Riding into Charles Street Station

In response to Joan Dobbie's "A City Wears Its River Like a Necklace."

The river wasn't yet someone else's necklace.
I glimpsed it on my way to work,
looking up from a book my boss had given me
about someone else's city.

Crew teams were scuttling home down the silver river
to breakfast and their first class, the mathematics
that would have freed me from electric typewriter
and telephone, from this two-hour commute
that ended at the ocean, the calculus
that would have kept me from
my residents and coworkers at Long Island Hospital.

I imagined walking alongside the river,
even just crossing it on foot
in sunlight that glittered on the water
like glass, like borrowed costume jewelry
and in the sunset that would stain it orange.

I imagined living near the river,
perhaps in the building I saw
right before entering the tunnel.
I would grow used to the sight of
trains before midnight and the black waters
after. The river would stay in my mind
the way that my aunt's gift of pearls did,
kept for special occasions, therefore
never worn.

But the river was always someone else's necklace.
I was passing through on a subway car
that was often filled with other riders
blocking my view of the river.
Most of them had a better right
to this necklace than I did.

The Last Summer without Air Conditioning

She sits on the porch
between the house and barn
with the friend who would
have been her landlady.

They sip OK Soda
from garnet goblets
as sun retreats into clouds
far from sunset or skyline.

The smell of grilled steak
rises from over the fence.
The Macarena bursts forth
from a car on Centre Street.

The neighbor with tiny glasses
slams his upstairs window shut.
His black guitar grinds and shrieks.
His mastiff howls.

The women pick at their salad
of dandelion greens
and avocado.
They will talk later.

She pretends that she can't
see her ex
ambling up the driveway,
but she can,
even over the gnash of guitar.

She pretends that she can't
see the city
that she is leaving,
but this is it,

the city that she is leaving.

Lafayette, September 11, 2001

Later that morning after classes were cancelled,
I crossed the river, beneath a perfect sky,
going home to you.

We didn't think that Al-Qaeda would reach us
in this college town,
this pin that the angels danced on.

We listened to the radio.

We thought about stopping by your parents'.
There your mother watched the news all day
as if it were the rain that would not fall.

Instead I watched the trucks trailing American flags
rush up and down Ferry Street,
making it a river we could not cross.

I wished it had rained that morning
while the passengers were lining up at Logan
and the workers were streaming from the subway.

Standing at the window, looking at the sky,
fierce even in Lafayette,
city of wedding-cake houses and candy stores,

I prayed for rain.

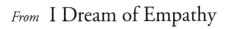

From I Dream of Empathy

Bethesda

The ghosts of green papayas
and used bookstores
haunt the chain restaurants
that rise up like
invasive flowers. Even so

these places cannot lose
the scent of lemongrass
and the brittle touch
of a yellowed paperback.

The specter of a woman
slips past the windows
of carefully folded cardigans
and the greetings
of the salesclerks who
already know your name.

No one notices this ghost.

The Jazz Harpist Considers a New Album

Dust settles on the silk flowers
fading in the endless summer
of asphalt and subcompact cars,
of weedy palms and blindingly
white bungalows.
These flowers remind her of
when things were less hopeful
in this California
that no one dreams of.

A friend's new LP plays.
He blooms in winter,
a saxophonist, a crimson orchid
in the time of black ice,
spiky branches, hard falls
up North, back East.

She herself may not live
until that season,
so she chooses to flower
now.

Augusta, Maine

I was made for the sun,
but here I am in Augusta.
At Christmas, the snow
is as real as ground glass,
and the Three Kings
are just statues,
less than the live dogs
around St. Patrick's manger.

All summer *mi hijos* played baseball
and I shivered in the stands,
drinking café con leche
from a thermos.
The sun gave no more heat
than a postcard of Florida.
My brown thighs shriveled
like bananas
left on the counter.
I covered them in mom jeans.

All winter I sit, huddled
indoors in a white parka
bought from a catalog.
I drink Café Bustelo,
straight, no leche,
my gloved hands around
a thermos from the bank.

Neighbors hike to the ski lift
on the edge of town.
The men balance six-packs
on their shoulders.
No one else winces at the wind,
the snow, the sleet,

the black ice,
the wind and the sleet
that pound at my windows
like someone else's bad lover.

My sons play hockey.
I keep them busy.
They are made for Augusta.

Babymoon

The young celebrity,
whom neither Lila nor her daughter know,
poses in her red and orange maxi.
She is on her babymoon
by the sun-dappled poolside
with real palm leaf cabanas,
banks of jasmine in bloom,
and lemon trees that cleanse
and sweeten the humid air.

Lila puts down the magazine.
She watches the pregnant receptionist
waddle back to the restroom.
That girl is the only worker
wearing flat shoes,
but they do match her red
baby doll dress
and drop earrings.
And her blond bob is sharp
enough to cut through
the salty, overcast day outside.

Lila sympathizes with her.
She was pregnant once.

During the long hot summer that began in April,
five months
before Estelle was born,

Dave offered to drive her
to the Cape
or at least Castle Island
to cool off in the tepid sun and salt breeze
heavy with warm onion rings,

beer, and classic rock,
to escape the city's stink
of garbage and perfume.

She turned him down.

When she was not at work,
she spent the summer upstairs
watching televised golf
for the cool greens and water hazards.

After The Summer of Young Men in a Hurry

The young men in a hurry played
all that summer in Manhattan,
the once black and white city
ripened beyond lavender into red.

The piano sounded
like storm clouds on the horizon
in a neighborhood
with only fans and open windows.

The high-hat shivered
like the taste of ice chips
about to melt.
The saxophone slipped

into the tightly-packed room
and across rough brick walls
like the last breeze
before September.

Listening to them, you wonder
how they would have sounded
in winter when clouds mean warmth
and storms spawn the fall of snow.

Summer Solstice on U Street

Let's pretend that it's midnight
as saxophonist Gary Bartz
steps onto the stage.
The room darkens;
candles on the table flicker.
Shadows hide the thickset men at the wall.
The ceiling lowers;
tiny lights strung above stand in for stars.

Imagine moonlight rippling on salt water.
The scent of mango dusted with
chili powder and cinnamon
trickles in with the piano and drums.
We taste fruits we don't know the names of.

Tap your toes, for sure,
or sway, following the pianist's lead,
but when the horn starts in again,
carry yourself a little straighter.
Cameras flash. Wedged in,
we are all caught in the glare.

All too soon imagine
the empty streets above.
Playing the last song, Bartz retreats
into the early morning's shadows,
the color of his long-tailed jacket,

and climbs the back stairs
to his refuge above the club.

When we leave by the front stairs,
it's still daylight on U Street.
We can no longer pretend.

The Jazz Harpist Lies Sleepless

At night in another strange bed
tiger-striped with streetlights
and shadows of venetian blinds,
the jazz harpist wills herself
to sleep.

Her husband sprawled beside her
is dead to the world.
She is alive to it:
the itch of wool blankets,
the whisper of a pink
nylon nightgown
over her thighs,
her place on the edge
of a full-sized bed,
the traffic like Pacific surf
outside her window,
the music she cannot
write down at night.

She imagines rising
to tidy up the room.
Her husband will wake
to a clear path
if only in this place.
She will not touch
the harp

that always
travels with them
like an awkward, half-grown child
looming over his parents,
the only child they will ever have.

She shuts her eyes
to this bedroom
and to her harp
that emerges in darkness.
She hushes her crashing thoughts
from the hours
most women her age
do not keep.

The music
and the darkness
recede
and she falls
into a dream
of willing herself
to stay awake
as her husband drives
her and their human child.

In her dream, she strokes
her little girl's hair,

and plays
The Look of Love,
as they travel home
long before midnight.

Evening on Chinkapin Street

The men are talking
about evolution, about relativity,
about earth science and epistemology—
how do we know what we know.

On a nubby blue couch,
I yawn, and the world blurs.
The night, half-heard words,
chirping music, and
the body, that ragdoll,
are all part of a dream
while the men are talking.

When I'm sitting with you,
our words turn the night to ocean.
We're stranded in a lighthouse.
Small oranges glow in glass bowls,
their scent and color brightening
this salty, mildewed room.

Finished with the visit,
we each take an orange
and go out on the porch.
I break off a vine branch.
Its last leaf rides the dry wind.
Dark cats depart the house.
I say goodbye to you drily.
There is no more ocean tonight.

November

November was the safest month.
The evenings came early. Mornings came late.
She rose in the dark, worked, and returned home.

The holidays lay ahead with their foods and feuds,
a banquet of mixed emotions, acid greens
staining the blue and white tinsel décor.

She could not imagine extreme weather:
summer's hands around her throat, knees on her chest
nor winter's treachery tripping her up at every turn.

She imagined a calm life with the one she loved.
They stayed in together. Apart,
they were planets, their orbits rarely meeting.

Yet everything ends when it ends.
Love is not the lease on an apartment.
A heart will stop alone.

This November, Wendy stands at her attic window,
looking out at the newly leafless trees, the empty street,
the cold sun, the full clouds, the short day.

Watching for what will come, willing her feelings to go,
she stands, a sharpened face in the muted month
that nonetheless, for her, promises sorrow.

Travels with the White Ghosts

As the two of them left the city,
flurries drifted onto the white car
like the ashes of a dozen term papers,
a hundred used books,
and a thousand letters from friends
burnt in a bonfire.

From the passenger's seat,
she looked back.
He grinned and kept going.
This was another good-bye,
another sack or two
of mail returned to sender,
another adventure
in a half-lifetime of them.
Only this time he
was in the driver's seat.

Together, the two of them inched
down the coast on back roads,
on dirt roads
through places where one could die.
They were escaping from a fire
down knotted sheets,
each one shorter than the last.

North of San Francisco,
they finally fell short,
landing hard in a small town.

Without him, a little pregnant
but not for long,
she then rode the bus east,
leaving the white ghosts behind.

Walking the Former Orange Line

Wendy walks the spine of the city
made of burnt umber brick
from tenements torn down after fire,
after renewal.

She walks beneath the canopy of unnamed trees
and sees people who look like her.
Two shaven-headed men
play tennis. Sweat glistens
on dark faces and white chests.
A woman, her head covered
in orange, blue, and brown cloth,
pushes her baby stroller past a couple walking dogs.

Wendy reminds herself that this is just a path
from one place to the next, from café to street fair
from school to home, for those who were not born
when this path was an elevated subway,
a scar running down the city's face.

My Mother Told Stories

Mother remembered cars with no radios,
so she told stories.
We munched on her favorite candy,
Necco wafers, the color
and flavor of spring-coat buttons,
muted pastels, pink gray white green.

She told stories
all the way past
the road to Whalom Park.
Its wooden roller coaster
(she said) had killed a soldier
just home from the war.

She told stories
as we crossed over
the Nashua River
that ran red
or blue or green
depending on the paper
Wallace's mill was making.
(As a girl in a pinafore,
my grandmother had waded in that water.)

Mother told stories as she drove
past the site of Mal's Goody-Goody
where she used to play under the tables
while the adults played bridge

and slipped the children
pennies and Necco wafers
to match their Sunday best
muted pastels plaids and checks.

Our mother told stories
all the way to Grandmother's house.
We sat in the front seat,
crunching the last of the wafers,
discs less sweet
than our breakfast cereal.
We hoped for more
but sometimes tasted
the pale licorice, pale lavender
that Mother recalled.

Green Corners Park

Every day the city is shrinking,
broken-windowed buildings that I knew
turning to green space,
the opaque river I remember
clearing, almost enough
to fish in,
not yet enough
to swim in.
The city is becoming
a park of trees and flowers,
lungs unstained by smoke,
tangy bark and mushrooms,
a symphony of smartphones
and car stereos,
rap and reggaeton,
bird song and bee buzz,
filling in the gaps
of my childhood memories.
Before work and after classes,
college students gather.

Javier and Rosa. Ary
and Sophea. Berhane
and Aster. Esther and
Alex. Jamal and Michelle.
Siobhan and Aisling.
Kevin and Kyle.

Every day the city is shrinking.
Our world expands.

Imagining Empathy

After a painting by Bea Garth

Looking at my friend's painting,
I see the two barefoot women
on the soft orange rug with a blue edge.

One is speaking. The other
cups her ear to listen.
A ginger cat balancing
on the couch's edge
adds his grace note to the women.

While one woman is listening,
the other is confiding something
about her husband or her children
born or unborn or her lover
about her parents or her job
about her body or her art.

I imagine the radio
purring like a second cat
while one woman speaks
and the other woman holding
a red apple hears her.

The windows reveal an aquarium,
fish circling the room.
They conceal the landscape outside.

They reveal only
the aquarium's warm salt water,
making this room a womb
where one woman entrusts
her observations to another.

She may be a friend.
She may be a sister.
She is not a lover or a husband.

Perhaps this is where
I should have been looking for
empathy all along.

Scene from the Blue Room

(1st voice)

Mrs. Feeney is dying in the room with blue walls,
the color of her favorite dress
from the summer she spent
dancing at the lake,
the color of her summer cottage there,
the ocean on the family cruise,
the sky the last time she saw Johnny,
and her granddaughter Olivia's eyes.

Once a large woman,
Mrs. Feeney shrinks from pain
in her tan and orange plaid chair,
the one that matches the white
that the walls used to be.
Her lunch of sugar-free, fat-free
vanilla ice cream melts
in its child's cereal bowl.
Only the broken pills persist.
Hot air blows in from the boulevard.
Cold air trickles from the fan above.
None of this eases her pain.

She supposes that she should be in bed,
if not at the hospital,
for that is where one dies
surrounded by beeping and tubes,
free from other people and pain.

That was where Jack, her husband, died.
That was where they could not save Johnny.

But she would rather be here
with her granddaughter
and the big band music
that sweeps in with the breeze.

Mrs. Feeney wants to hum the music
the band played at the lake
all that summer.
She wants to start
her sentimental journey soon,
at the blue hour,
the hour when the dance begins.

(2nd voice)

Twenty days late, Olivia holds
Grandma Feeney's cold, blue hand
and tries to say something, anything.
Even if it's not about
the cruise. Or the cottage
before the glittering lake became
a slimy pond with weeds and glass
before her father died.

"I miss…," Olivia whispers.

But Grandma is shrinking.
Her eyes closed,
she is pulling away.
Soon she will be
just like Olivia's father,
someone she will try hard
to remember
in other places, some of them
rooms with blue walls,
some of them near the water,
most of them not.

"I miss…," Olivia whispers,
remembering early mornings
in the blue kitchen
by the lake.
Mornings her mother rushed to work.

She wonders if she should feed
her grandmother.
She wonders if she should answer
her vibrating phone.

"I miss…," Olivia whispers,
thinking of the guy she met
six weeks ago.

Olivia bites her lips,
tastes the blood in the

lip gloss. Its sweetness
already makes her sick,
as sick as yesterday's soup
or today's milky cereal
made her.

Even the vibrating phone in her pocket
makes her sick.
Only this melting ice cream doesn't
make her sick.

She wishes she could be
dramatic, compelling her mother
to listen, pulling on her hands,
the way her friend Mandy would.
She wishes she could widen her eyes
or at least catch her mother's gaze,
the way Mandy could.
But even if she looks and talks like her,
even if she goes to church with her,
she is not Mandy.

"Blue is such a spiritual color,"
Mary Rose Feeney says,
flipping back her blond hair.
"The color of the Blessed Virgin.
No wonder why it causes
you to eat less!"

Olivia knows she will do
what her mother recommends.
The phone stops
like a beating heart.

"I will miss. . .," Olivia whispers.

Olivia is shrinking.
She is pulling away
into her body,
ignoring the sickly scent
of her mother's vanilla candle,
sensing only the dull headache and nausea,
praying for the twinges
and flow that will bring her back
on time.

Grandma's eyes are closed.
Olivia wishes that she could
hold her father's hand again
hold her grandma's hand again
as they walked out of the cottage
to the lake that sparkled in the sun.

No,
she wishes
that she could hold the hand
of the child that is growing
inside her,
waiting for the world.

(3rd voice)

After walking in from the garage,
Mary Rose Feeney stands, arms akimbo
in the middle of the living room.
She would curse
the hospice workers and the blue walls
if ladies cursed.

And she is a lady
in a cute white top and
floral jeans and with
tiny toenails painted pink.

She has sold many houses.
She sold one today,
right before pulling into the driveway.
But she remembers
how hard it was
to sell the cottage
at the lake,
actually, a pond
no one ever goes to anymore.

She shivers, remembering her plunge
into the slimy, olive-colored water.
She was sure that the rocks were
broken glass and her feet were
cut-open and bleeding.
No one else swam in this lake.

No one even sat on the porches
of the tiny houses ringing the lake
like takeout boxes around a lawn.
Only she plunged in.
That was always what happened,
even before her husband, J.J.,
could not be saved.

Before the priest arrives,
Mary Rose lights
a syrupy vanilla candle.
She is warding off
the smell of death,
unwashed yet not unclean.

"Blue is such a spiritual color,"
she chirps
as if she really meant it.
Her mother-in-law and her daughter
think she does.

She knows she does not.

She leaves the living room.
Her phone is ringing.

It's not the priest.
Someone else wants to sell
a parent's house.

Walls can always be painted over.
She knows they can.

Harbour Round

after a photograph by G. Tod Slone

The ghosts of houses stand
on boulders and pale shrubs,

green fingers sprouting
in the absence of people

and the hard, needled trees
that sprout up inland.

The blue-gray houses fade into the sky.
Paint dissolves in years of salted mist.

The wood disperses into watered-down light,
no longer bearing weight or pain.

This was once someone's home.
But in the next photograph,

give or take a few years,
one will see only the rocks, dirt,

and trees pricking the summer air
flecked with black flies and sunlight,

all that persists in Harbour Round
once ghosts of houses fall.

She Wonders What Will Become Of This City

The sky above swells into a bruise over a blood vessel.
Swarms of mosquitoes rise from puddles and gutters.

It is always about to rain, sometimes about to thunder.
Acid rain cannot cleanse the ground or the air.

The pages of books dampen and thicken,
becoming too heavy to turn, too blurred to read.

The green fuzz of moss grows over trees
like plaque on teeth. Bones ache with decay.

Buses stall. Last year today would have been Code Red.
No one walks. No one rides for free.

She wonders what will become of this city
when oceans rise and ghost towns form like coral reefs.

The real coral reefs will have crumbled,
all color leaching away into the corrosive sea.

She wonders if the people huddling miles inland
will ever visit the abrasive waters

and imagine what might have been
in the ghost town where she now sits.

Or will they avoid the scouring waves
and build their lives on mountains, now islands

above the waters, above the swarms of mosquitoes,
above the trash of daily life in a ghost town?

From Listening to Electric Cambodia,
Looking Up at Trees of Heaven

Listening to Electric Cambodia

Tiny ants invade your house,
spilling over the window sill.
The ceiling fan stirs the air
until it's as warm as your beer.

Ants speckle the sea-green tile floor.
The organ swirls
as the girl in the lemon dress
steps up to the mic.

Glowing, she sings in Khmer.
It is 1967.
She has no worries.
She is sixteen.

She will not live to see thirty.

A Paralegal in DC

I am allowed to wear red or white
but not
orange or peach.

I am allowed to eat in the break room
but not at my desk.
I am not allowed to date
coworkers.

I have become translucent,
but I no longer need sunscreen.
Spring and summer are rumors
seen on a webcam.

Only the receptionist has flowers,
scentless orange and peach,
fresh, not silk.

Hands up my sleeves, I wonder
where all my time in this city has gone.

Once She Was a Subway Flyer

Addison Road was the end of the line.
Beyond here there were only buses
the C29 down the highway
past strip malls, past farm stands,
past the DMV and the gas station,
to the front door of the college.

She was a moon-faced girl
in black among the masked faces,
her students coming from work,
the stout security guards,
and the boys to men
with blank white shirts
and shorts past their knees.

That was nearly ten years ago.
She looks like her mother now,
tightening a gunmetal belt
over a navy cardigan.
She walks to work.

Someday she might come back
to see what this place has become:
the new town center, the stores,
the station
a village green with
Kenny the mayor on Foursquare,
Addison Road,
no longer the end of the line.

The Tree of Heaven

I butt my head through
concrete. I defy
polluted soil
studded with glass.

I drink poison.
I squeeze through
fences.

Together with
rabbits and feral cats,
I colonize the park.

It is illegal to plant me.

In China, my roots and bark
become medicine
to cure baldness.
I am the tree of heaven.

Of Music and Metaphor in Somerville, MA

Putting her flip phone on vibrate,
Lila considers her ex, Dave.
He reminds her of an album cover.

Out of the sun, he keeps his colors
(more or less)
but he is not new.

She herself is a CD, smaller,
her case a little cracked
but, inside, not the worse for wear.

Their child Estelle
is a downloaded song,
mysterious, fragmentary, free.

Rose of Sharon

One summer, just after she took out the lilac bushes to appease my aunt, my grandmother planted a Rose of Sharon tree in the front yard. My brother and I called it the Stick of Sharon because it was just a stick— no leaves, no branches, no flowers. The Nashua River flowing through downtown was more colorful, turning red, yellow, or green, depending on the dyes used at the mill that day.

The next summer Gram sold the house and moved out to the country with us.

Every so often I Google her old address. Only two houses remain on Avon Place, a dead-end street less than a mile from downtown and the once-colorful river that will someday be clean enough to swim in. My grandmother's house is green now—and the Rose of Sharon, almost the size of the other trees, flourishes. And the lilac bushes have grown back.

All About Rosie

Whenever I imagine Rosie, she is always
racing
up and down the stairs of her building,
out to Little Italy,
mingling with the famous people
who aren't quite famous yet.

The pink record player is on full blast
in the living room
as she washes up last night's dishes.
Horns sound like the traffic below.
A blind man tickles the ivories
so that they sound like ice clinking.
You can barely hear the flute
over the splashes and running water
although Rosie swears it's there.
Just you wait!

Rosie always wears what we call vintage,
red belted dresses that fit just so over slim hips,
stilettos that won't break.
Her blonde pixie cut's never mussed by wind.
She spritzes the smoke-filled rooms
with White Shoulders.

She is a real Size Ten.

When Rosie is working,
she sharpens pencils,

hits carriage return on a manual,
serves coffee to the men from Detroit,
engineers who will play Jazz for the Space Age
on the latest hi-fi's.

She quit smoking. Or she didn't.

The music in the clubs became
the music on her husband's stereo
became the music of your life
became the standard this
girl in purple sequins is singing
at the piano on the memory-care ward.

Once again Rosie's a real Size Ten.

Grosvenor

This was the future.
Towers rose
in shades of grey
metal glass and concrete
above the boxwood
and evergreen grass.
Come inside.

The future smells of curry,
collard greens,
and canned soup.
Its walls feel
chipped and greasy.
The future needs
fresh paint and new carpeting.

New tenants
enter the elevator,
their arms full of
chocolate-colored bedding,
polka dot pillows,
tinsel for a white Christmas tree.
It is their future now.

Night Train

I.
Rain rattles the roof
of the night train going north.

A dozen people under umbrellas
wait twenty minutes for the last Metro.

Lightning flashes
over the ocean.

Last buses arrive and
depart.

II.
The night train going south
presses on into Sunday morning.

We pass the green beginnings
of the river that divides the city.

The great-grandmother in jeans checks her cell phone
while the grandson no longer in uniform sleeps.

This will still be the night train
after we leave,

when the river ends in seawater,
and morning is lost in afternoon.

The Real Antarctica

In the real Antarctica,
the tiny cruise ship sneaks between
the stony gray beach and the icebergs.
Below the water seems dark,
lifeless.
All the same
Lynne Cox once swam here.

A single man sits bundled up beside her.
The summer sun sheds much light,
no heat.
This is not the Antarctica she imagined
during the winter she lived in Brooklyn,
the winter she burned dinner
every night.

Another hot flash races through her body.
Deliberately, she throws off her hood,
tosses her gloves aside.
She unzips her parka, unfurls her hair.
She strips down to a t-shirt and jeans
and waits for the ice shelf to crash.

Walking Past Mt. Calvary Cemetery in Winter

The snow melts under soft gray skies.
Even now it clings, like cobwebs, to corners.

The holly hedge's red berries and sharp leaves
hold the eye until the next snowfall.

Geese graze for grubs on the hillside.
The size of toy ponies, they do not fly.

Just like the waxy magnolia, the spiky cypress,
the leafless, last black locust,

they persist.

Somewhere in the city a woman on a patio
spoons sorbet. The nearby quince blooms.

Somewhere a bronze nude on a tabletop confronts
the indoor birds of paradise, the outdoor bittersweet.

They too persist.

The River Always Captures Me

The Blue Line train crosses the river—
on one side the city,
the power plant, and rows
of brick houses, on the other,
the park with its paths
like veins of a broad leaf.
Below a tiny figure walks
a tinier dog. Someone else
bikes alone. No one rows
yet.

Soon the river will begin
to smell like spring.
More people will walk its paths.
Then it will reek like summer,
a regatta of rowers sweating,
dogs dripping,
tadpoles dying in
drying mud.
In fall, the leaves
will cover the ghosts
as the last rower skims past.

Still later the flat opaque water
will freeze in patches.
From the matching sky,
snow will fall
past the tiny figure

and the tinier dog
that trace the paths
that are like
veins of a leaf
by the river
below the Blue Line.

The Music of Her Life

Julie London quit her day job today.
No more half-sunny, half-smoggy mornings
standing around the set,
holding a clipboard, sipping coffee
from a vending machine,
nursing a sore throat, fighting with the brass.
No more smoking in the break room.

Back in their high-rise apartment,
with the view of rush hour,
she shucks off her nurse's cap;
her white lace-up shoes;
her matching uniform,
that knee-length, zip up carapace;
her powder-white opaque hose;
all onto the white shag carpet.
She keeps on her pink girdle.

Tonight she will sing "Cry Me a River"
once more on stage.
She will wear black sequins again.
She will glitter
while Bobby leads the band.
The audience's drinks will sparkle,
the colors of her eyes and hair.

Chicory

All summer I stay outside.

Even when the grass blanches
to straw in sunlight,
I bloom blue.

I stay strong
when the air is like bus exhaust
and the sky is a dull ache.

As the humidity bears down,
I spring up green.

I am what the children want to be
as they ride their bikes over the lawns
up and down the block.

I never go inside.
I never wilt in cups or vases.

No one civilizes me.

Find Your Beach Where It Is

I.
In Greenland,
children play past midnight
on a rocky beach
without sand or seaweed.

Nearby flowers and lichens appear,
brightly wearing down boulders.
Tourists' tents bubble on sand
like orange and green fungi
on a fallen log.

They do not squander summer.

II.
The children in New England
fling ribbons of brown seaweed
and streamers of green
back into the water.

Adults swaddled in
gift store cover-ups
avoid the Atlantic's bite
and the seaweed that clings
to every wader's legs.

III.

The young father and his sons
fish from the banks of the river
his grandfather swam in.
It was clean. It was decent.

Sun sparkling on the water,
the green flourishing on the bank,
the white of new polo shirts,
hide dangers in the fish
that swim this river
the color of a memory.

At the Museum in the New City

We watch the Detroit train station crumble,
its eighteen stories buckling, time its wrecking ball.

Green and black graffiti invade like ground ivy or kudzu.
This could be Chernobyl. Only cockroaches scale these walls.

At the next panel, Trees of Heaven mulched with schoolbooks
burst through the floor and up to the roof.

Brick houses collapse like ice in hot water. Nevertheless,
the face of the owner on the abandoned BBQ joint welcomes us.

Even if each leaf on each tree is transformed into a poem,
how many times can we watch a city fall apart?

New Poems

New Moon

We can't follow the new moon.
It hangs in the smudged sky
cleared of clouds.

Already setting, the moon
shows up on our way home.
It's been hidden all day
while we've been watching
thunderclouds pile up on the horizon,
a storm that never happened.

The new moon is leaving us
like the airplane taking off
for Chicago or California,
maybe even Japan.
Venus lingers for a time,
standing in for the stars
we cannot see.

Within the Realm of Bagels

The yoga teacher lights incense
to dispel the scent of
bagels baking below.
For a moment I imagine

having stayed on in Queens,
having grown a harder shell,
a mint-green spring raincoat, makeup,
willingness to do aerobics even
if I hated the music,
hated the sweatbands and shorts.

I picture myself living
in a studio, a niche
in a knick-knack cabinet
of plaster figures: the social worker
married to her job, the teacher
with his backpack of papers,
the accountant retired at fifty.

Would I be here now,
following the incense's wavering scent,
following my breath.

Or would I be below, breathless in
a twenty-year old spring raincoat,
sipping black coffee to remain
within the realm of bagels.

At the Renwick Gallery's Exhibit on Burning Man

My husband disappears, replaced
by someone wearing a t-shirt
advertising a motorcycle repair shop
in Cloverdale, California.

I don't panic.
I immerse myself in this other life.

Adorned with a headdress
made from bottlecaps,
wearing a white nylon slip
to match the mountains,
I dance in the heat
that I have always shrunk from.

A younger, bare-chested version
of the man from Cloverdale
stomps to the sound
of empty half-gallon jugs
and cafeteria drums.

In this world,
I ride on the back
of a motorcycle.

Wind chimes gather around,
protecting us.

Working with Stone

After Racconto, LS2, Bice Lazzari (1958)

In this story, the canvas becomes
stone. The sky turns the color
of concrete. Clouds, black scuffs, emerge
once you squint. Sun trickles down:
wan pink, not orange, not red,
not light revealing blades of grass.
The shadow is a wall, concealing
grass, dirt, cigarette butts coated with
slick lipstick, broken glass, candy wrappers.
Disembodied, a white jacket floats free.

After Bice Lazzari's Racconto n. 2 (1955)

As if written on birch bark,
the story is mainly white space
but with an erasure
at its heart.

But red tear stains streak
onto the leaf of a new book,
one bought to escape
love lost, a city gone,
art abandoned.

Beneath the surface, figures form:
self-portrait of the artist as a size ten,
her curves hidden in a stiff wool coat;
the wall she and her husband
breakfast behind.

A New Englander Listens to Pet Sounds

Listening to the crinkle of a detuned guitar
like sunlit leaves
on narrow roads,

so far from California's highways
around lizard-like mountains
basking in the parched sun,

I remember

riding with my uncle and my father
past maple trees, past stone walls,
past abandoned tractors in fields.

Poet on the Subway

I can't write in public.
I'm not that thin girl
hunched over her moleskin notebook,
bearing down with Bic pen,
filling up pages with miniscule
print, crisp phrases, line breaks.

My handwriting bloats, falls down,
falls apart, not clutching the
pole, not toeing the lines
as the car shakes and
passing people clip my hand.

When I was that girl
hunched over, I was reading.
I remember riding all the way
to Union Square just so
that I could finish my book.
Co-workers said I'd be mugged
if I kept doing that.

I imagined riding to Brooklyn,
losing myself in Balzac, stopping
at line's end, Coney Island
at night, the summer's finale
in sour and bitter indigo.

There I'd pretend to wait
for another train, one leaving
for anyplace other than this
city, anyplace other than this
life where I was that girl
hunched over, not writing.

In Another Life, We Live in Presque Isle, Maine

North of the mountains,
winter winds and spring fog sweep
over the pond and through red pine,
swaddling us as we read and grade papers,
tying us to this place.

Summers I wander the downtown
the small towns of wide streets and storefronts
he wanted to escape from, the ones
I wanted to escape to for a little while.

The daily Greyhound from New York City
crawls into our town. A former student
or two emerge, coming back from the city
of subways, museums, Japanese gardens,
vendors selling oranges and helados,
the city of raised voices, sudden rain.

When I come home, my husband is listening
to all the old music on YouTube,
the songs he used to have on vinyl.
Everything stopped in 2005,
the year we moved here.

We talk about going back,
but tonight the stars come out,
stunning us with far more
than we could see back home.

Tomorrow morning,
the fog will roll in with dawn,
binding us here
to this place.

Facing Worcester

Myself a compass
needle, I face
north towards my birthplace,
the antique
hospital on one

of seven hills
in the city of spas,
piazzas,
parlors, and tonic,
words no one uses

anymore. I face Rice Square's
African
cloth stores, bodegas,
and Indian
fonts on bags of rice and

red lentils,
remembering the
Polish nuns who
fought Grampy on how to
say his name.

I face the city
of Water Street,
barrels of dill half-sours,
Kosher soap,
hipsters' whiskey bars.

Flying into Warsaw in Another Life

In this life, the eastbound airplane
simply hangs above the toy landscape:
cotton ball clouds; tiny, nameless trees:
the ocean, a smooth, dark sheet
without trash or fish or shipwrecks.

Tomorrow morning I land in Poland,
my grandfather's country, country of trees
with yellowed leaves and peeling bark,
of cobblestones coated with cigarette smoke,
of lumbering oxen and steam trains,
of people who look like me
but swish and swallow vinegary consonants
that burn going down an American's throat.

In this life, I don't know
that Grampy never lived in Poland.
In his own village, near Vilnius,
his words, a foreign language, swirled
like wood smoke in morning air.

We Never Can Live Where We Want

A friend's ashes clump by a red bush.
His quizzical, bearded ghost
peers in at interns opening mail.

He had been happy once
as he wandered by the river
drinking bad coffee.

But I feared being caught
scattering his ashes
into slow, black water.

I feared clambering
over rusted shopping carts
while police watched above.

Now my ghost can't leave town,
ashes mingling with the cat's.
Our urn is the pin

upon which I, no angel, dance.

Dinner at Larry's Restaurant, Cambridge, MA

I've never dreamed about
meals I ate at Larry's,
dim walls steeped in soy sauce
and ginger, the same light
each winter and summer,
no music, no talk, just slurp
of hot and sour soup, tap
of chopsticks on thick plates.
I was the only one
who used a fork, who strayed
outside the sciences'
precise light, the only
white woman in the room.

Often I ate Mapo
Tofu there. White cubes stood
waist-deep in umber sauce,
hint of ginger, hint of
anise, no taint of sweet,
not deep-fried like tofu
served to white ghosts.

Often I drank bitter
black tea. I filled my cup,
a thimble, once again
while I clung to my seat,

still waiting for the man
I liked to join me there,
his rapid talk breaking
the dim restaurant's spell.

The Letter I Never Wrote You

Last night I dreamed we were
never really friends. Your spicy cologne
and cigarettes, the smell of antibacterial
soap, kept me at a distance.
I'd never see what you wrote
in fountain pen on yellow paper.

I'd never sit next to you,
never eat your Tulsa Trail Mix,
never get drunk with you on
spiked egg creams at your house,
never invite you to my room,
never even ride in your car,
the one you would soon total
going home to Durant, Oklahoma.

This time you offered to teach
me to drive stick shift. Laughing,
using your accent to charm me,
you would even offer a ride

out of this college town where
I am a fat moth pinned
under glass in the butterfly museum,
where I choke on small print
and fast food, where I'm alone.

But this time I knew you.
I knew all that would happen.

I said no.

On Drawing the Six of Cups

Snow-covered spruce, my age-mates, surround me
as I walk the long-gone path,
once dirt, trodden-down grass, and stone,
now asphalt. Ghosts of ponies linger,
breath rising and mingling with mine.

Beneath tall pines, bronze needles lie
as if no snow fell today,
heaping onto stiff spruce, bare trees,
bleached grass, and stony fields alike.
A toy stove, still aqua and
white, remains below. Plastic, it will
persist long after the trees will
be felled, long after I'm gone.
I look for a sword but find
only dolls, only a white bear
in a yellowed hand-smocked dress.

A mountain appears in this country
of old hills. I climb it,
drawing on strength I never had
when I lived here or in
the country of mountains. Following paths
that never existed, I push through
the evening to see this place
for what it was and myself
for what I wish I'd been.

Maryvale Park 2019

A red-winged blackbird hangs and sways
on last year's reed. Gray fluff still clings.
New reeds unfurl, not yet quite tall
for this or any other bird
who swoops and calls in flight.

A deer stalks through the swamp,
but I await last summer's turtle,
creature that I mistook for stone.

The minnows' school is bustling
downstream past empty bottles
of water and Tropical Fantasy
from our lottery stores.
The left behind, one fish flirts
with rocks, with bottles' mouths.

I wonder what will remain here
as climate changes, as oceans rise:
mosquitoes rising from algae bloom,
trim women walking robot dogs
they will not outlive,
young men guzzling soda and dropping
bottles in the swamp
as deer slip in and track this path.

Why We Left the Forest

Riding into the heart
of the forest, all we
found was worse than absence:
unburnt brown soil, splinters
of wood, remains of trees,
of shade, mushrooms, and moss.
No birds called past us.

We walked, paced really
on levelled ground, too hard for
bare feet or Chuck Taylor's,
just right for steel-toed boots,
shoes my brother would wear.

All we saw were hills of
the same as far as we
could see. Again, we were
too late. Again, we turned
around. Next year we would
be back east, once again
in our Jerusalem.

Facing South

Brackish waters invade the coast,
even under sunny skies. Ground
sinks and dissolves. Streets become
streams, boulevards rivers, yards ponds
or lakes. Only parking lots
resist for a time. Jellyfish
and seaweed occupy the city.
Skyscrapers remain, their windows closed
against thick, rancid air. Houses
built on a human scale
float off, join the garbage
patch mustering in the ocean
where no one sees them.
Humans retreat, their new normal
in the mountains. Their children
build floating cities to stand
their ground amid rising tides
of water, seaweed, and trash.

The Indoor Sculpture Garden

After Sara Parent-Ramos' exhibit "However Because"

Objects from the sea
surface above
sea-level. Vibrant blues
shimmer, form
patterns, speak in code.

At this party,
humans are mingling with
ceramics.
Some know each other.
Most don't. I clutch

my phone, dancing in and
out of this
game in which we guess
the other's names.
Speechless, objects glisten,

the vanished
artist's nameless children,
hidden from our
winter world of mud and
pelting rain.

After October

Written in the brilliant corner
of a living room, his poems
once climbed up the wrought-iron
bookcase, past his father's albums,
past his friends' books, past his daughter's
picture to the world beyond.
There his words still breathe, racing
like raindrops down a summer window,
rising like smoke from the last century's
jazz clubs, mingling with the notes
that Monk and Parker had played.

Tonight, at the crowded cafe,
a young musician sits at the piano
in front of the painted skyline
that appears to be New York,
not the city of parking lots outside.
Like the leaves from street trees,
the man's notes shake free in the wind.
Brilliant colors scatter without
anyone to write them down.

Music in a Spring of Wind and Rain

Piano notes and drum beats flow,
a waterfall contained in a courtyard.

I imagine a friend, a jazz poet, listening to this
while his lizard-like mountains bask in fierce sunlight.

The music he heard at their feet was smoke and ash,
rising from parched ground, permeating hair and skin.

Words drifted through like trash or tumbleweed
while smoke hovered over parched ground.

Fountains had been shut down.
Only pennies remained.

Outside the courtyard where I sit,
rain plunges down the hotel's façade.

Everything I hear is water.

Midsummer Moonrise

After "Midsummer Moonrise" by Dwight William Tryon (1892)

At first glance, you see
just prettiness,
a haze of green, flurries
of brushstrokes,
scent of turpentine.

Be patient.
Yellow and white flowers
appear, plants
for which you've no name.
You might know them

as you walk past them. Or
you might not.
The gash of silver
water opens
up, reflecting chalky

moonrise, yet
water does not dis-
solve this parched moon.
With time, you see needles
on pine trees,

copper blight elsewhere
as wind rifles
through. The gash of water
widens. You
smell the earth at night.

Van Gogh's Les Racines Seen in Summer

Beside a window out to a world covered in leaves,
these roots express winter,
the winter we will soon have this far south.
Not the northern photographs of
marble snowbanks flecked with sun, stiff jade pines,
and pearly-pink skies decorated
with empty, lacy trees. But this winter
in black and white, brown and gray,
of pencil, ink, and black chalk.

In August, we are headed to the paper-colored
river tinged with stray chalk from trunks and roots.
The empty tree stands stark on the bank.
It commands attention while turpentine
pervades the air. Ghosts of other trees
curl up like smoke. Sunlight
is a thin, brown wash, not cold
but warm.

Color returns with spring, flecks of yellow
and green, scents of mud and water,
carrying us back to August
when these roots are exposed.

Facing East at Dawn

After a photograph by Northscapes Photography, Presque Isle, ME

The driftwood is a hand grasping something
then letting it go. Stars scatter above
as if this hand, not God's,

had tossed them into the morning sky.
Up there, they grow brighter. They will
fade once lemon sunrise washes away night.

Yet there is light now. Stars band
together into the Milky Way. Clouds form
like clusters of maple leaves clinging to water.

The water is itself. It reflects nothing.
It rests beneath the sky, awaiting sunrise
and its long day as a sparkling mirror.

It contains everything: cans, rocks, hornpout, weeds.
Before dawn its splash on the shore
is quieter. No birds break its surface.

Across the lake, someone's car rounds the curve
from the next town nearer to sunrise.
Its light is a fallen star. Soon others will follow.

Facing East at Sunset

After a photograph by Northscapes Photography, Presque Isle, ME

The photographer turns away from blaze
of orange light and burnt clouds
to the side that could be
dawn or the beginning of night.

Filters stain this sky and pond
sapphire in the blue hour, not
quite night but evening. It's November,
just past four on a Sunday
out on Chapman Road in Maine.

The photographer thinks of Frost's pony
jingling through woods south of here.
These woods are silent; no cars
lumber by, flashing lights at him.
The dead trees harbor no birds.

The trees stand like the ruins
of a house never finished, burnt
in the west's fire. Bleached grass
piles up like ashes, heaped beside
the pond. The north wind blows
through, rattling empty milkweed.

Yet the photographer stays, waiting
for stars to appear like rain
that quenches fire. He waits to
take their picture.

1979

After Herbie Hancock's "Finger Painting"

Piano notes drift
like dancing snow
along the Charles River.
Orange light
drowns out the last stars.

Concrete towers,
Harvard's red-brick buildings,
thick hedges
conceal the city.
The notes won't stick.

Melting on asphalt, they
turn to rain.
Drivers stop and start.
Ten years ago
Armstrong walked on the moon.

Now it's too
far. It's easier
to imagine
caravans leaving town
while snow falls.

In this world, the sky
belongs to birds
and clouds alone. Drivers
without stars
follow the river.

Of Blessed Memory

After a photograph of Holocaust survivor Flora Singer

The sun bleaches the slats
of a black and white fence.
Small statues bask

in sunlight, not too warm
on this October day
just before leaves turn.

You stand in the space
cleared from matchstick woods,
a place far from home,

the woods you looked out to
from the Catholic orphanage,
the woods you wandered

while in hiding. Surrounded
by the frog musicians
of Grimm's fairy tales,

your back to the ash leaves
about to turn
the color of old bruises,

you have no more stories to tell.
You look out to the camera.
Now you are home.

Seven of Stars

I do not seek Death.
Lovers do not call out to me
as I wander through the city
where the flute and fiddle
trickle down steep steps.
No one here holds
the tarot card I seek.

On this card, yellow globes blossom
on lettuce-green trees. The barefoot man,
blond hair curling down a coarse neck,
peers at this fruit, too-sweet lemon,
somehow growing so far north
that herbs weaken,
tomatoes are evil,
and sunlight washes
bitter, yellow ink
over a paper sky.

The Fool ignores me. The Magician,
concerned with his cloak, withdraws.
I must leave the walled city for trees
with fruit, music from automobiles.
Witches have always lived here,
but without magic or money,
without the Seven of Stars,
I cannot.

From the Roof You Can See Forever

His voice sounds like a swallow
of pure lemon juice, no sugar.
You choke as it goes down
and the studio orchestra swells.
Acid waves creep onto cold sand
as the garden dissolves in rain.

You try to remember if this
is Lennon's voice, long silenced.
You wonder how he would sound
as an old man, bent, bald, blind,
his son long grown. Still smoking,
he'd be a remnant of the old
city on the new island of
purified air, ringtones, vapes,
iced coffee infused with nitrogen.

Men like him live in fifth floor
walkups, crowded with hardback books,
vinyl records, cigarette butts, coffee cups.
Halting, they climb to the roof,
awaiting what the city will become
once the asphalt-colored rivers rise
and the island dissolves in rain.

In the City of Churches

She spent all Sunday not finding one
as if they had all raced ahead
of her plodding path, as if
her younger self had wished them away.

Instead the streets brought her cafes,
old cookbooks in Polish, a zoo
of toothy animals, dark red flowers
crushed on the sidewalk.

She thought she was dreaming,
passing a wooden house,
fading yellow amidst the brownstones.
She wondered if the church

she'd find would be wooden as well,
its stained glass made of tissue paper,
its priest with his back to the congregation.
He'd speak Lithuanian, not Latin.

In this church, there would be
no organ, no choir. Six or seven people
from her family's black and white photographs
would loiter in the pews as the night hung on

the last notes of a hymn.

Acknowledgements for New Poems

Bold + Italic – "1979" (also nominated for Best of the Net)

Bourgeon – "Flying into Warsaw in Another Life" and "The Indoor Sculpture Garden"

Duane's PoeTree – "Within the Realm of Bagels"

The Ekphrastic Review – "Van Gogh's Les Racines Seen in Summer"

Eyedrum Periodically – "Facing South"

Firefly – "The Letter I Never Wrote You"

Mad Swirl – "Facing East at Dawn," "Midsummer Moonrise," "We Can Never Live Where We Want," and "Working with Stone"

The McKinley Review – "*After Bice Lazzari's Racconto n. 2 (1955)*" as "Working in the Fifth Element"

Mermaid Mirror – "In Another Life, We Live in Presque Isle, Maine"

One-Sentence Poems – "A New Englander Listens to Pet Sounds"

The Pangolin Review – "New Moon"

Pisarze.pl – "Music in a Spring of Wind and Rain" as "Muzyka na wiosnę wiatru i deszczu"

Ppigpenn – "From the Roof You Can See Forever"

The Ramingo's Porch – "After October," "At the Renwick Gallery's Exhibit on Burning Man," "Dinner at Larry's Restaurant, Cambridge, MA," "In the City of Churches," and "Why We Left the Forest"

Setu – "On Drawing the Six of Cups"

Sycorax Journal – "Seven of Stars"

Verse-Virtual – "Facing East at Sunset"

Write Like You're Alive Anthology 2018 – "Facing Worcester"

Writing in a Woman's Voice – "Of Blessed Memory" and "Poet on the Subway"

Young Ravens Literary Review – "Maryvale Park 2019"

About the Author

Marianne Szlyk is a professor of English and Reading at Montgomery College. She also edits The Song Is..., a blog-zine for poetry and prose inspired by music (especially jazz). Her first chapbook, Listening to Electric Cambodia, Looking up at Trees of Heaven, is available online at Kind of a Hurricane Press. Her second chapbook, I Dream of Empathy, is available from Flutter Press and Amazon. Her first full-length book, On the Other Side of the Window, is now available from Pski's Porch and Amazon Her poems have appeared in The Ekphrastic Review, of/with, Loch Raven Review, Bourgeon, Mad Swirl, Setu, Solidago, and One Sentence Poems as well as in anthologies such as Music of the Aztecs and Resurrection of a Sunflower, a collection of responses to Vincent Van Gogh's art. The poet and editor Anna Maria Mickiewicz has translated two of Marianne's poems into Polish. She lives near DC with her husband Ethan Goffman, an environmental writer and wry poet, and their cat Thelma.

CPSIA information can be obtained
at www.ICGtesting.com
Printed in the USA
BVHW082149060820
585580BV00002BA/321

9 780975 309575